From Dad, with Love:
31 Lessons for my Daughter

© 2025 Smart Star Books & SmartStarBooks.com. All rights reserved.

Author: M.J. Cove

Published by: Smart Star Books

ISBN: 978-1-968207-03-8

No part of this publication may be reproduced, stored in a retrieval system, or transmitted in any form or by any means—electronic, mechanical, photocopying, recording, or otherwise—without the prior written permission of the author.

Exception: Only individuals and family members have permission to reproduce pages for personal use.

Some illustrations and design elements in this book may include AI-generated components. All compiled content is original to this publication, and the author retains full ownership and use rights for both personal and commercial purposes.

For more books and resources, visit: www.SmartStarBooks.com or search on Amazon.

Smart Star Books, 120 State Avenue NE, #138, Olympia, WA 98501

www.SmartStarBooks.com

About this book...

Author, M.J. Cove has designed this book to share personal and loving thoughts from fathers to daughters.

Each section has a challenge prompt for a father to write personal notes in an open-ended box to his daughter.

On the bottom of that page are some quotes to ponder and touch emotions.

On the opposite page, one of the 31 lessons are presented. There is also a short note to avoid certain thoughts and behaviors, offering wise advice and loving warnings.

10 Words That Describe You...

1. _____
2. _____
3. _____
4. _____
5. _____
6. _____
7. _____
8. _____
9. _____
10. _____

My dream for you is...

"A daughter is one of the most beautiful gifts this world has to give."

— Laurel Atherton

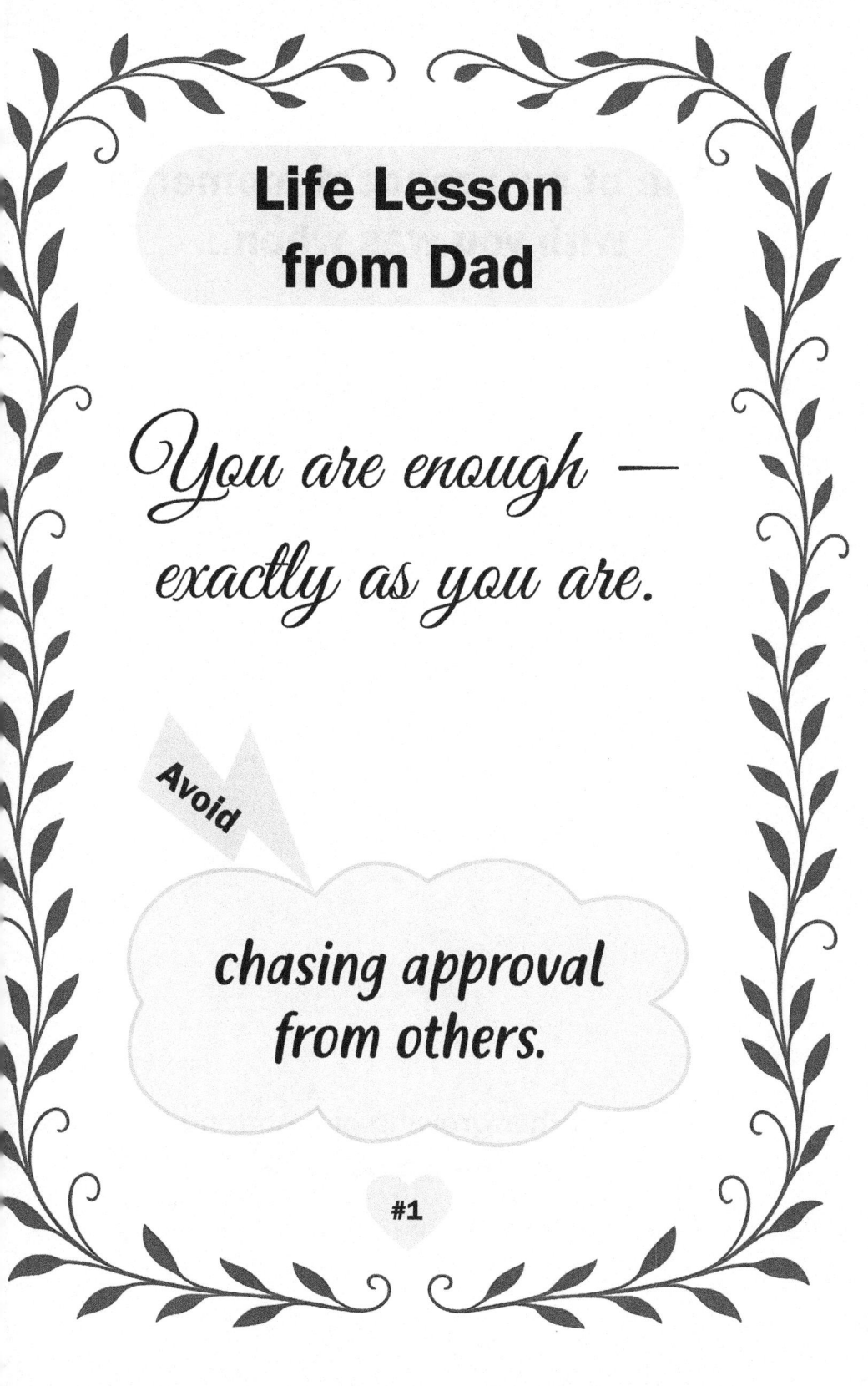

One of my proudest moments with you was when...

"To a father growing old, nothing is dearer than a daughter."
— Euripides

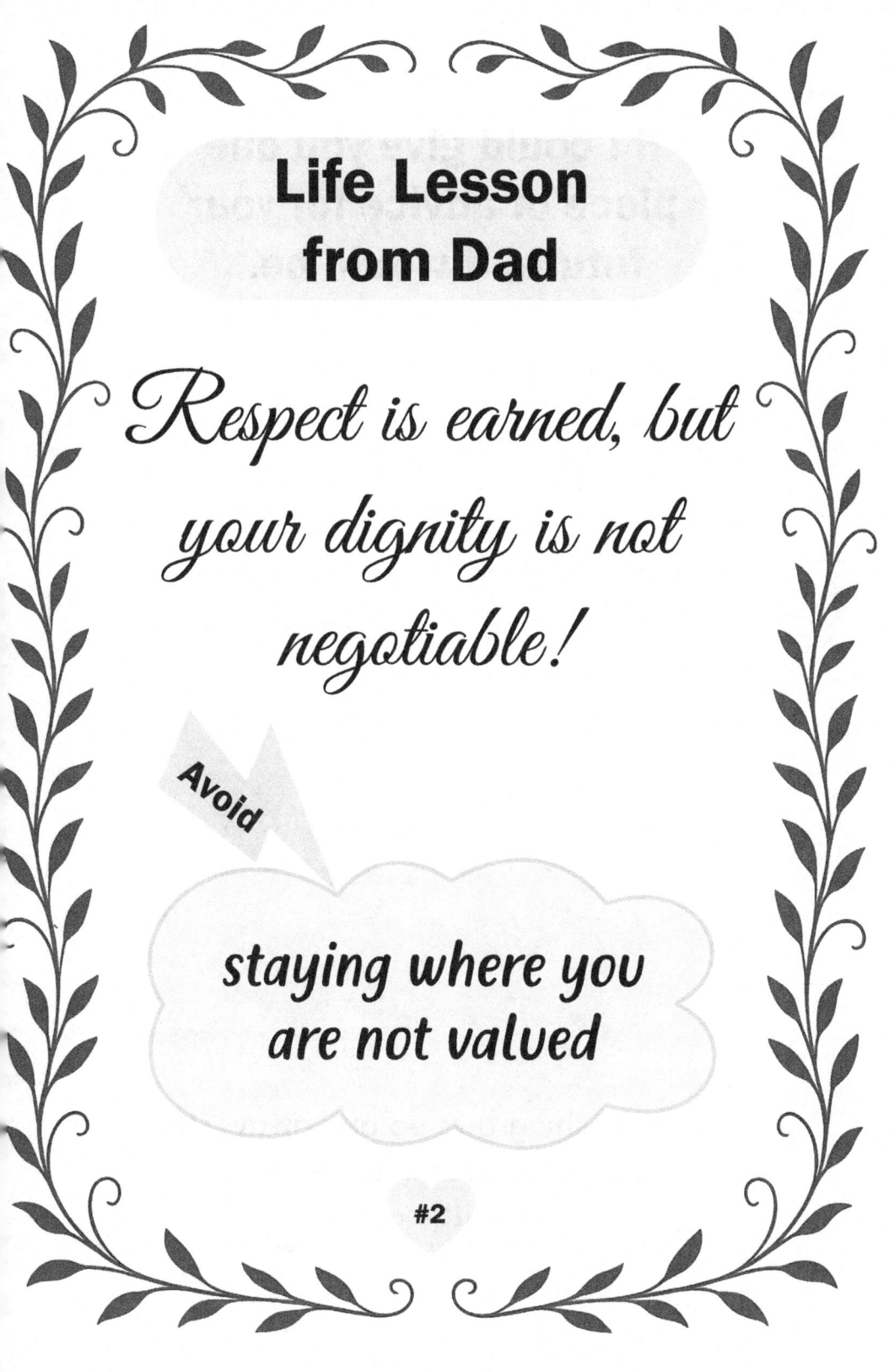

If I could give you one piece of advice for your future, it would be…

> "Even as she grows up and away, she'll always be close in my heart as my little girl."
> — Unknown

Life Lesson from Dad

Your voice matters. Use it.

Avoid letting failures define your future.

When you were little, you always used to...

"A daughter who knows her worth through her father's love won't settle for anything less."
— Unknown

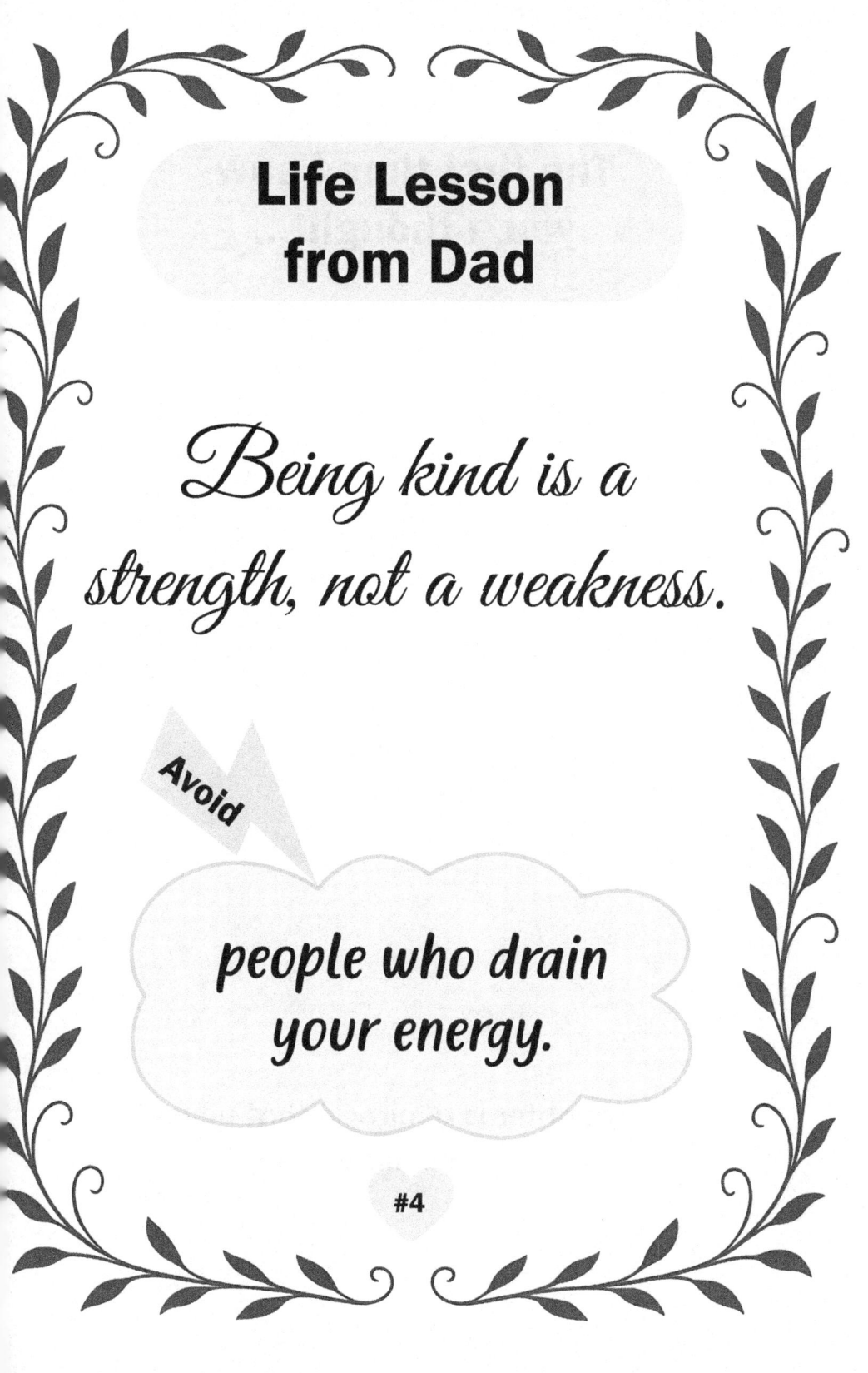

The first time I saw you, I thought...

"A daughter is a miracle that never ceases to be miraculous."
— Deanna Beisser

Life Lesson from Dad

Learn to say no — and mean it.

Avoid comparing yourself to others.

#5

One thing I hope you always remember about yourself is...

"A daughter is the happy memories of the past, the joyful moments of the present, and the hope and promise of the future."
—Unknown

Life Lesson from Dad

Your body is your home. Treat it with respect.

Avoid

gossip — speaking it and listening to it.

I see your strength when you...

"A daughter is God's way of saying,
'I thought you could use a
lifelong friend.'"
— Unknown

Life Lesson from Dad

Love is not supposed to hurt.

Avoid spending more than you earn.

#7

What I admire most about you is...

"Daughters are like flowers that fill the world with beauty."

— Unknown

A funny memory I'll never forget is...

"A daughter will always be the girl you treasure, and the woman you are proud of."
— Unknown

If life ever gets hard, I want you to know...

"When my daughter says, 'Daddy, I need you!' I wonder if she has any idea that I need her far more."

— Stanley Behrman

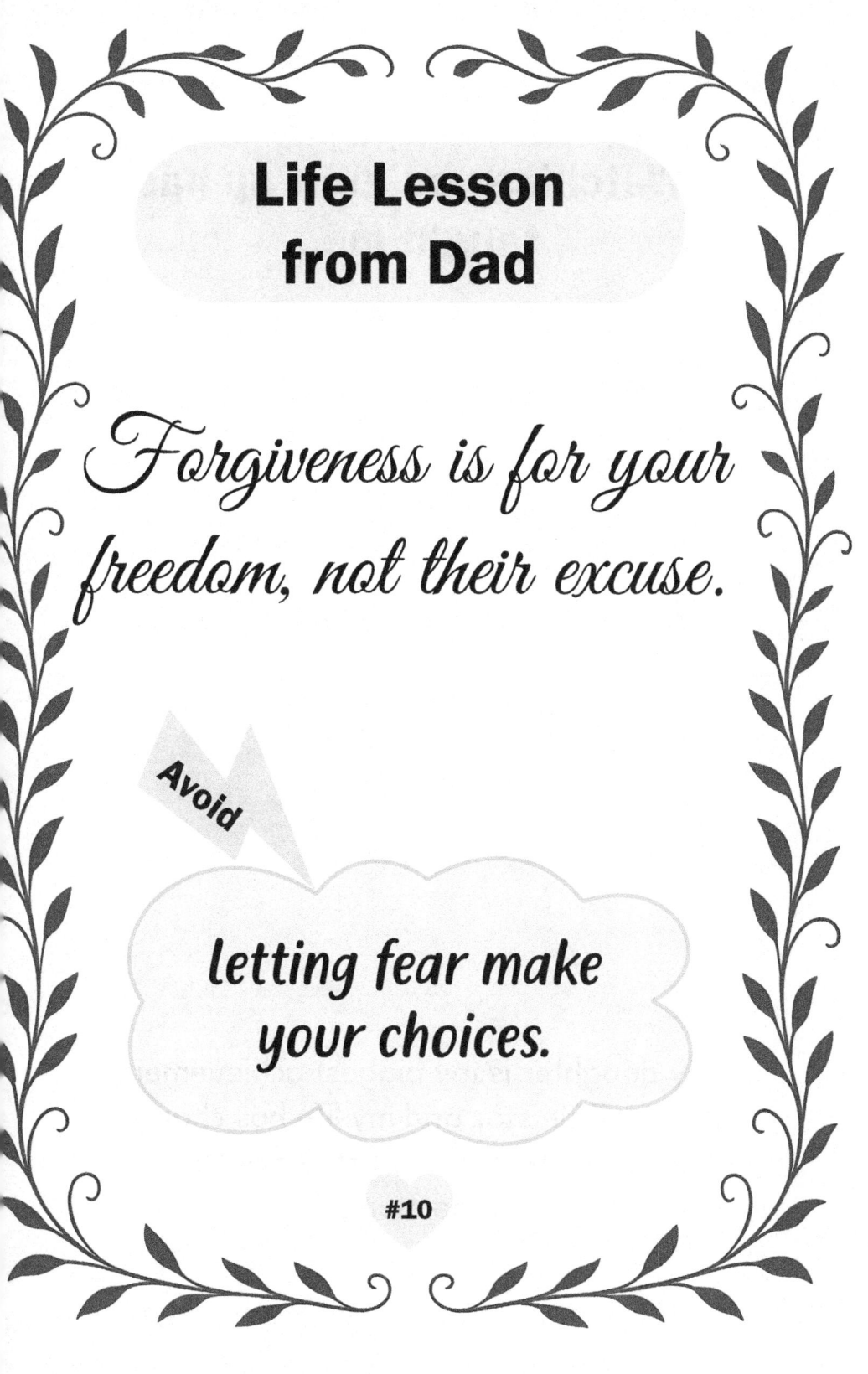

Watching you grow up has taught me...

"My daughter is my biggest achievement. She is a little star and my life has changed so much for the better since she came along."
— Denise Van Outen

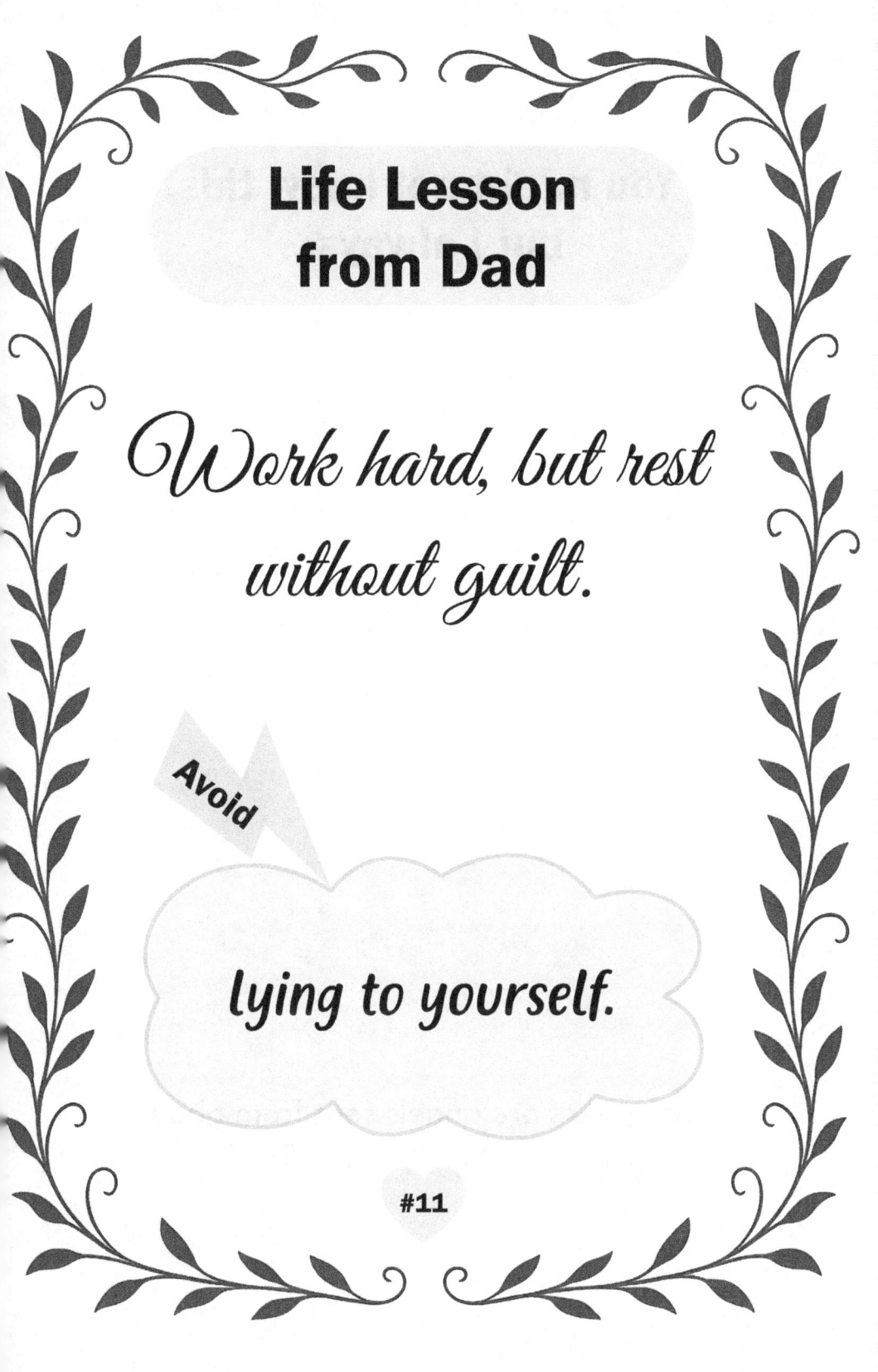

You might not know this, but I always...

"Daughters are angels sent from above
to fill our hearts with unending love."

—J. Lee

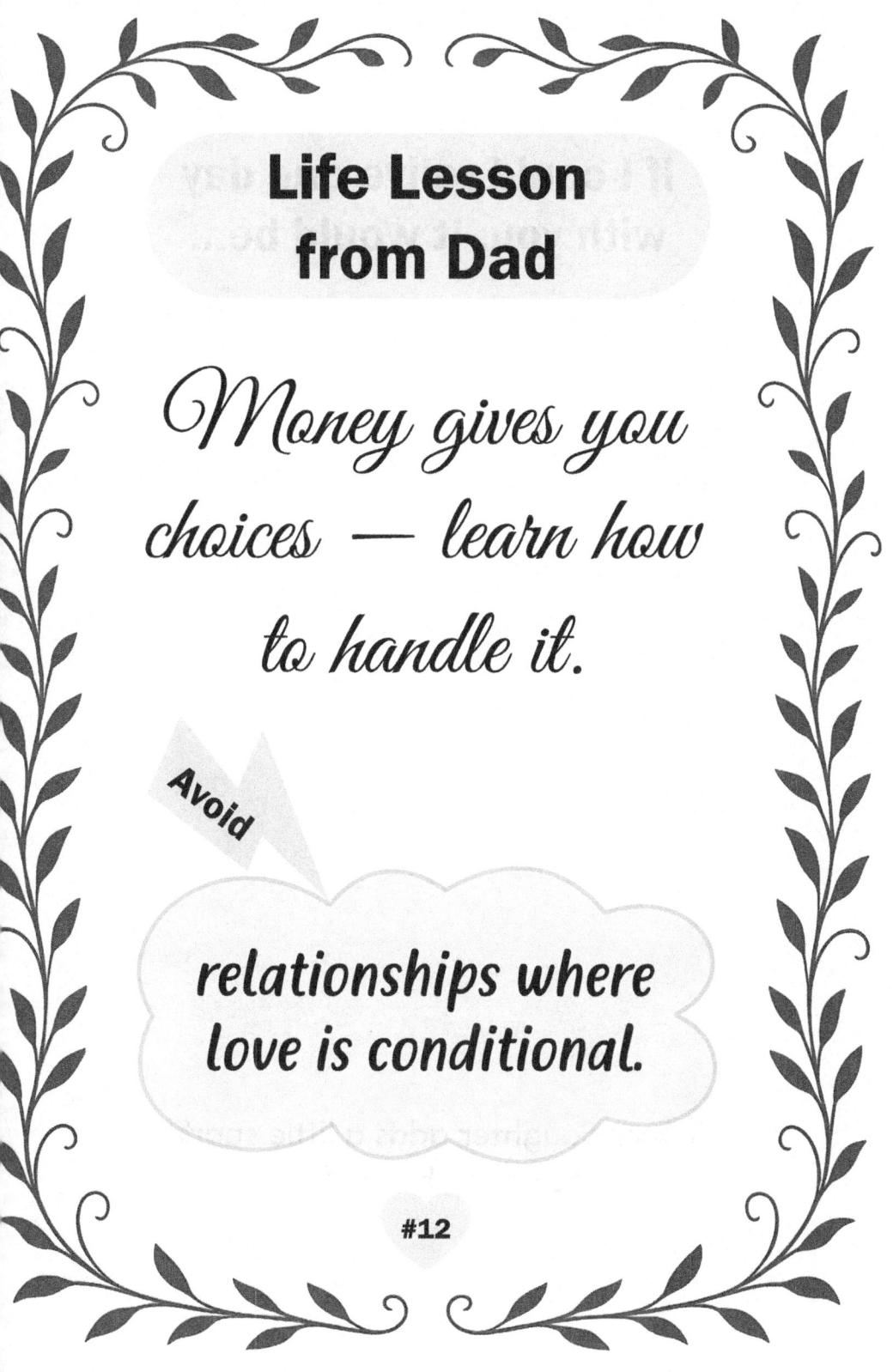

Life Lesson from Dad

Money gives you choices — learn how to handle it.

Avoid relationships where love is conditional.

#12

If I could relive one day with you, it would be...

"Every daughter adds a little sparkle to her father's life."
— Unknown

Life Lesson from Dad

People will remember how you made them feel.

Avoid revenge.

#13

I see a lot of myself in you when you...

"I hope my daughter grows up to be beautiful on the inside, rich in kindness, and generous in spirit."

— Unknown

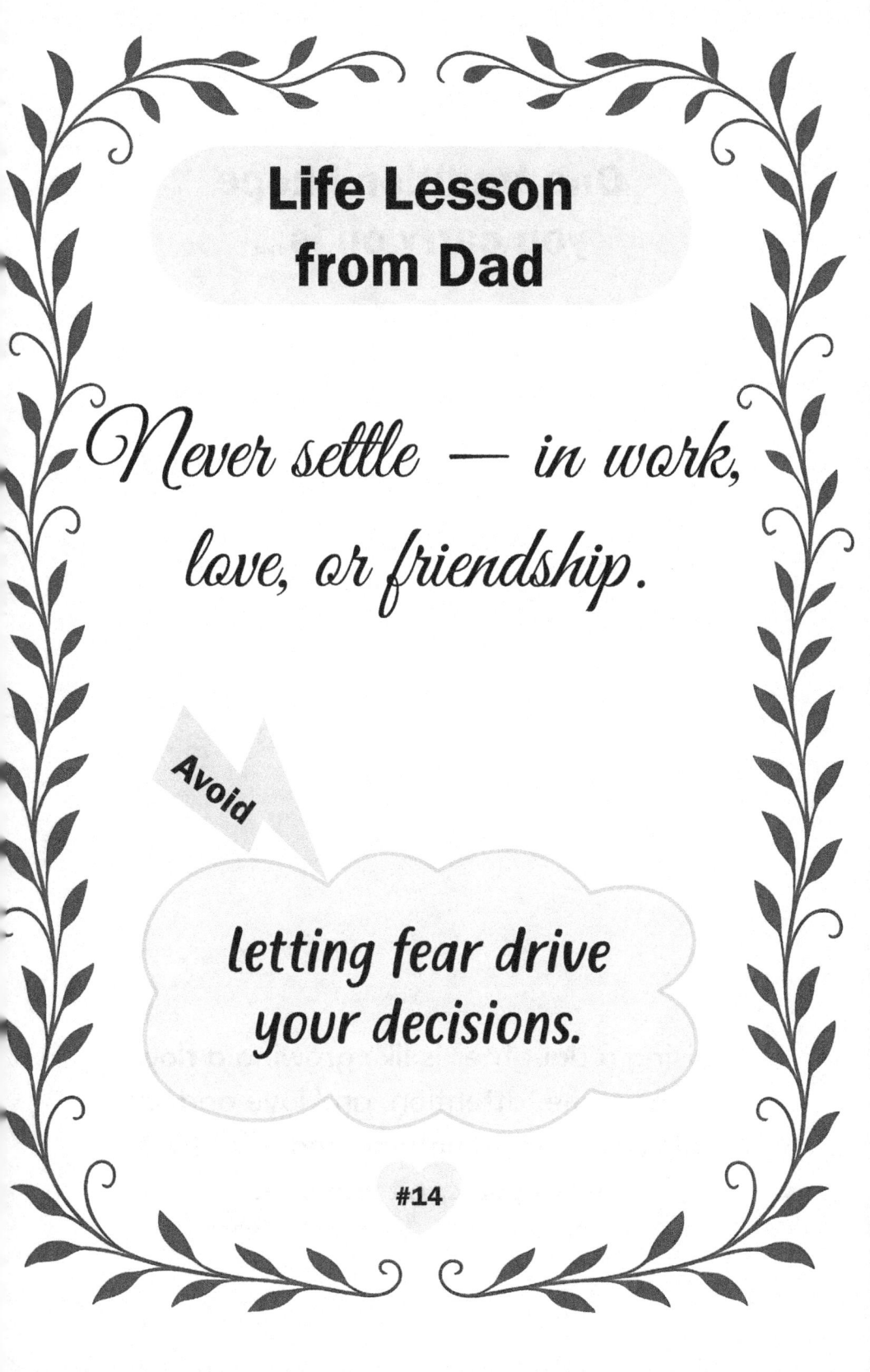

One tradition I hope you carry on is...

"Raising a daughter is like growing a flower. Give her time, attention, and love and she'll blossom into something beautiful that even you can't imagine."

— Unknown

Life Lesson from Dad

You don't have to fix everything or everyone.

Avoid relying on others for your happiness.

I knew you were growing up when...

"Little girls soften their daddy's hearts."

— Paul Walker

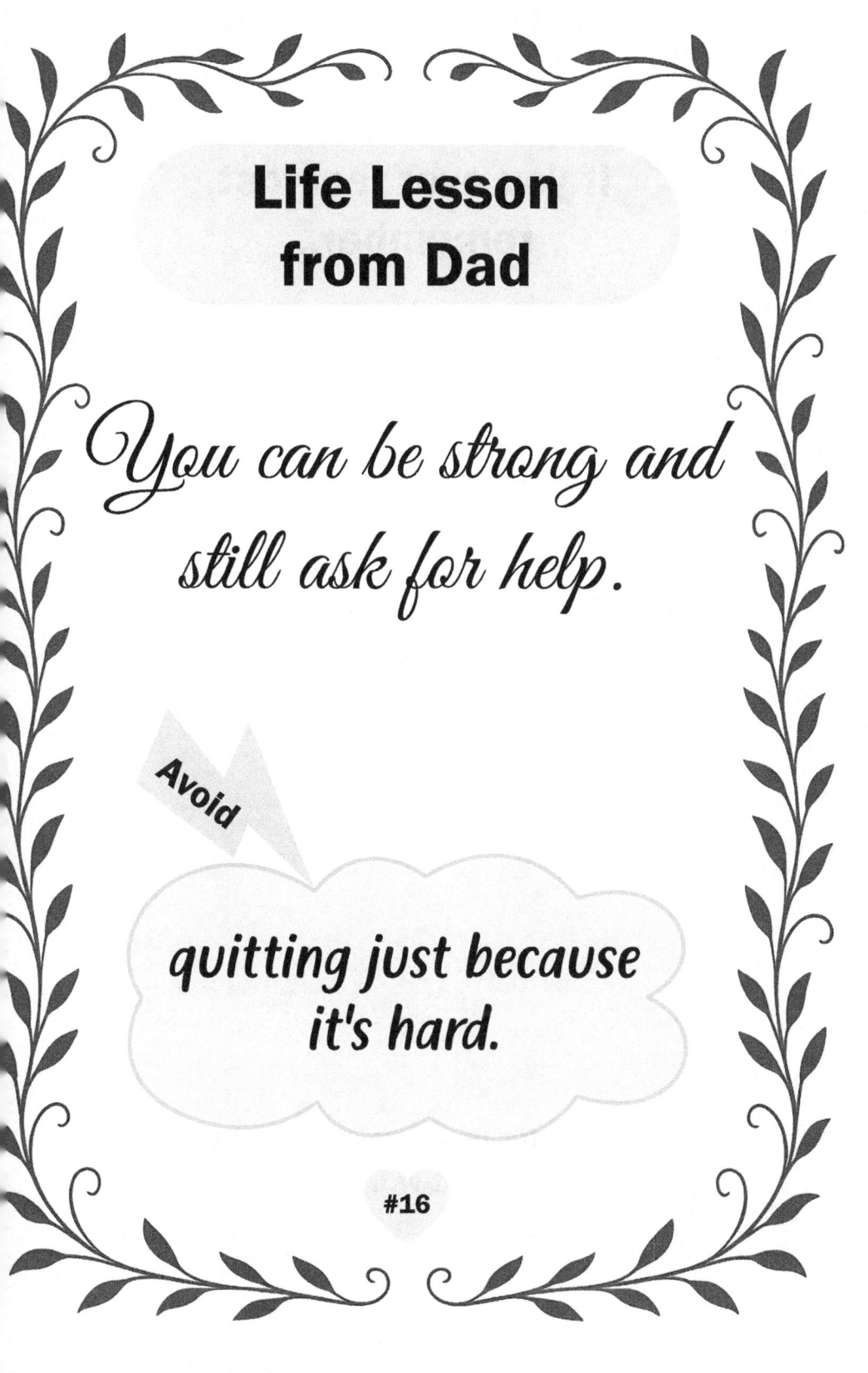

If you ever feel lost, remember...

"A daughter is a day brightener and a heart warmer."

— Unknown

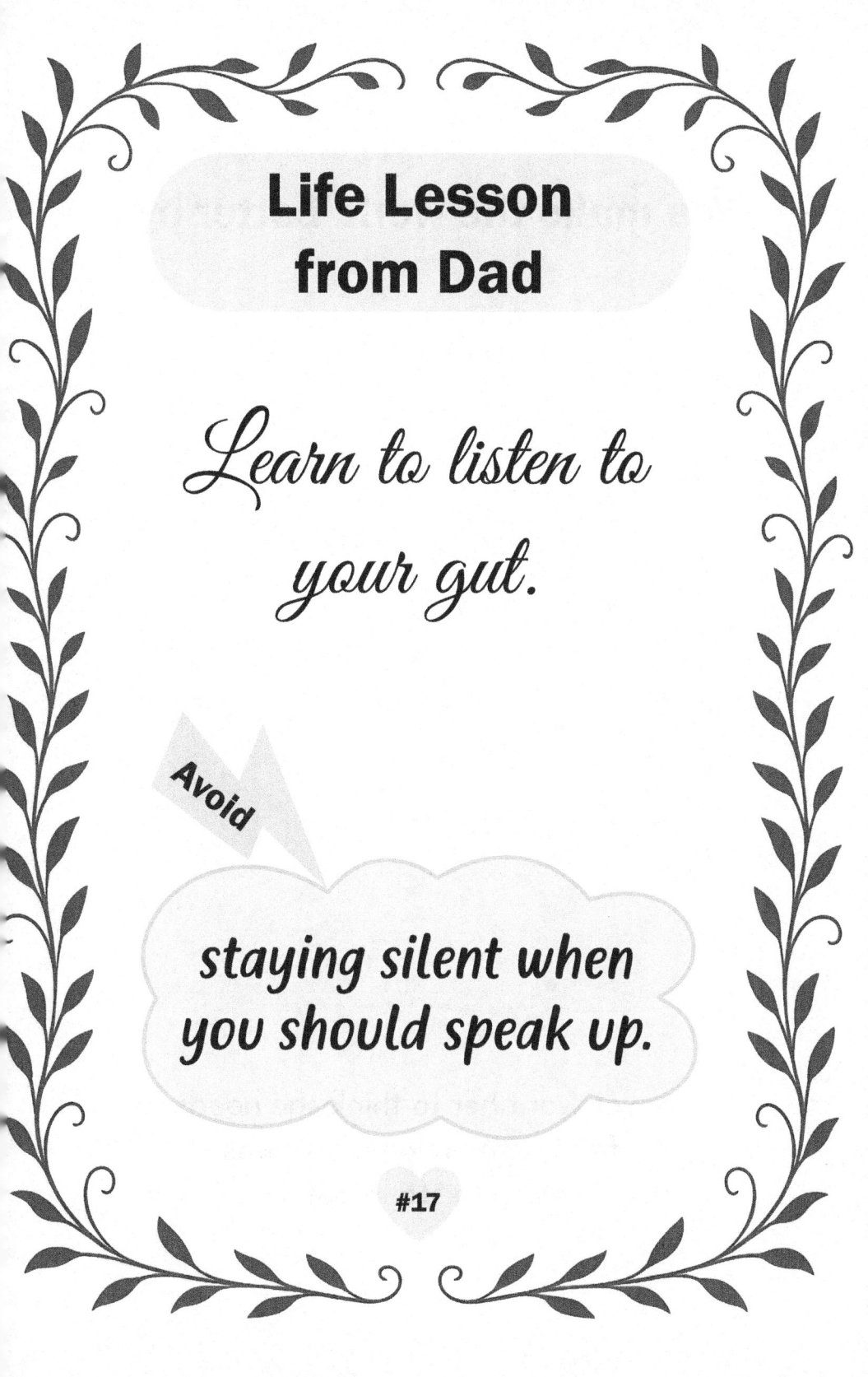

You make the world better by...

"I never want her to think she needs to
fit in with anyone. She was
born to stand out."

— Unknown

Life Lesson from Dad

No one else gets to write your story.

Avoid anyone who makes you feel "less than."

#18

I hope you always chase...

"Daughters are like snowflakes—each one is unique and special."

— Unknown

Life Lesson from Dad

You will never regret being honest.

Avoid ignoring your health.

#19

One lesson I learned the hard way (that I want you to avoid) is...

"I see the best parts of myself in my daughter. She makes me want to be better every day."
— Unknown

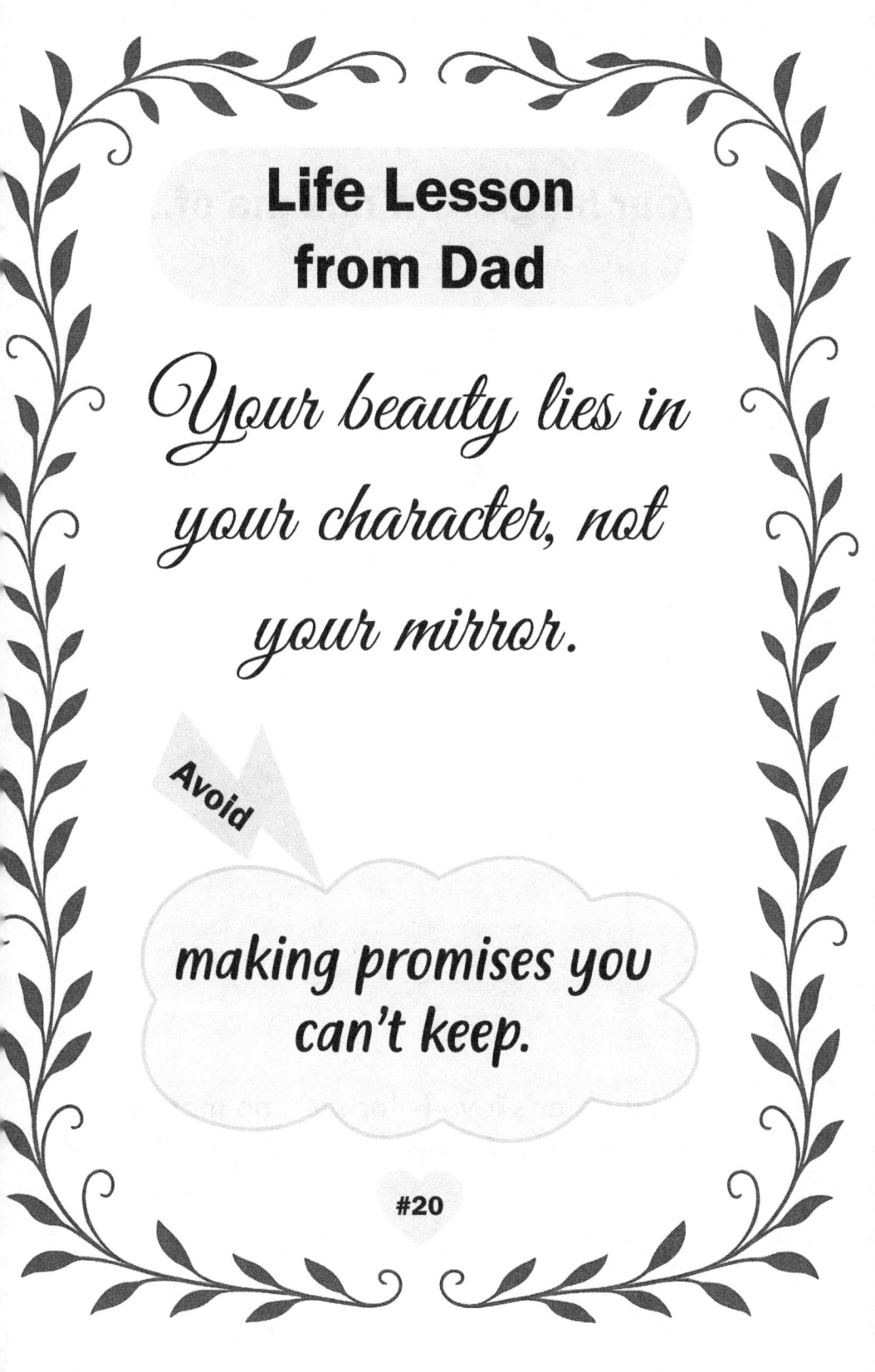

Your laugh reminds me of...

"A daughter's love is forever, no matter how near or far apart you may be."
— Unknown

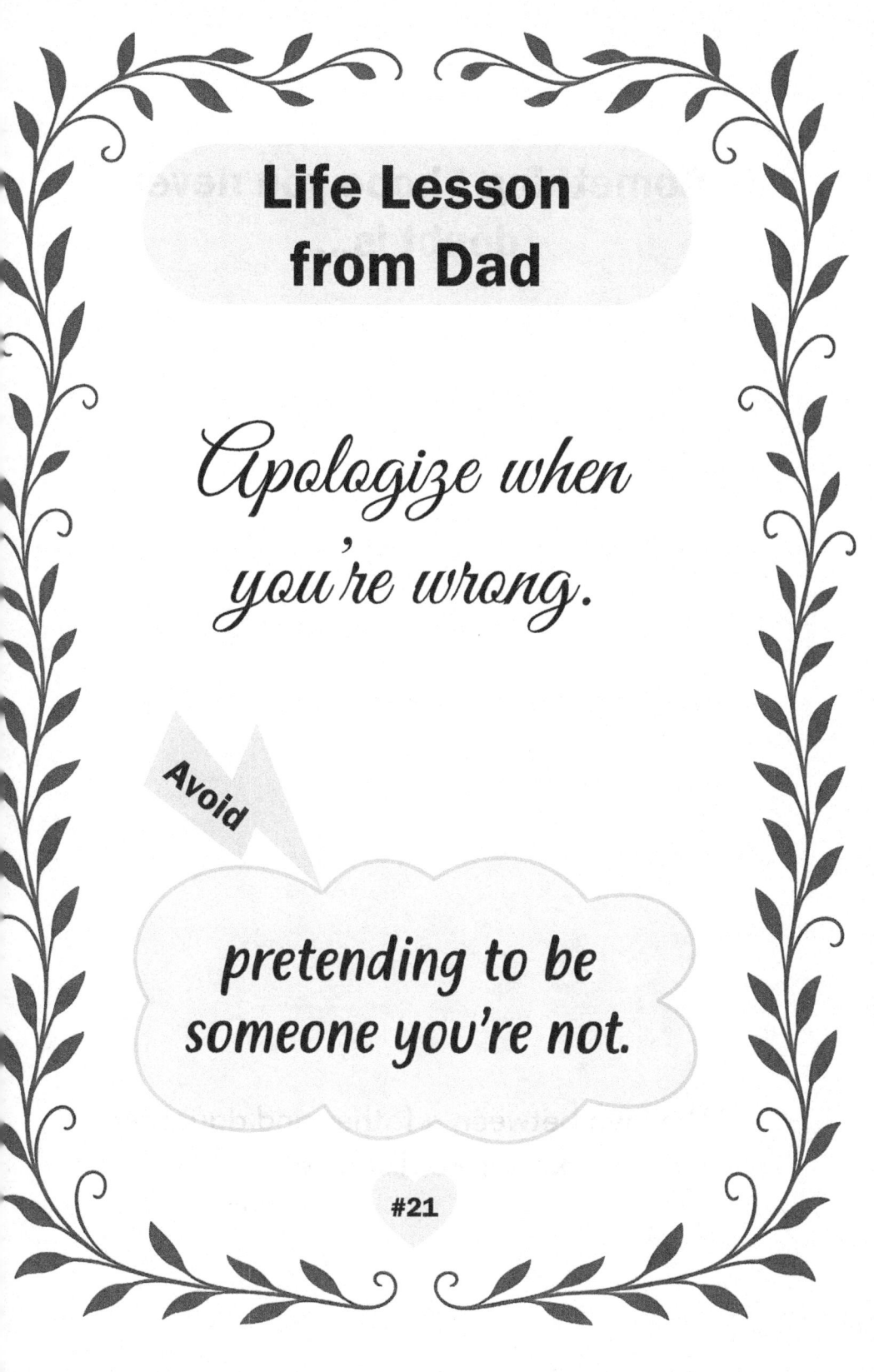

Something I hope you never doubt is...

"The love between a father and daughter knows no distance."
— Unknown

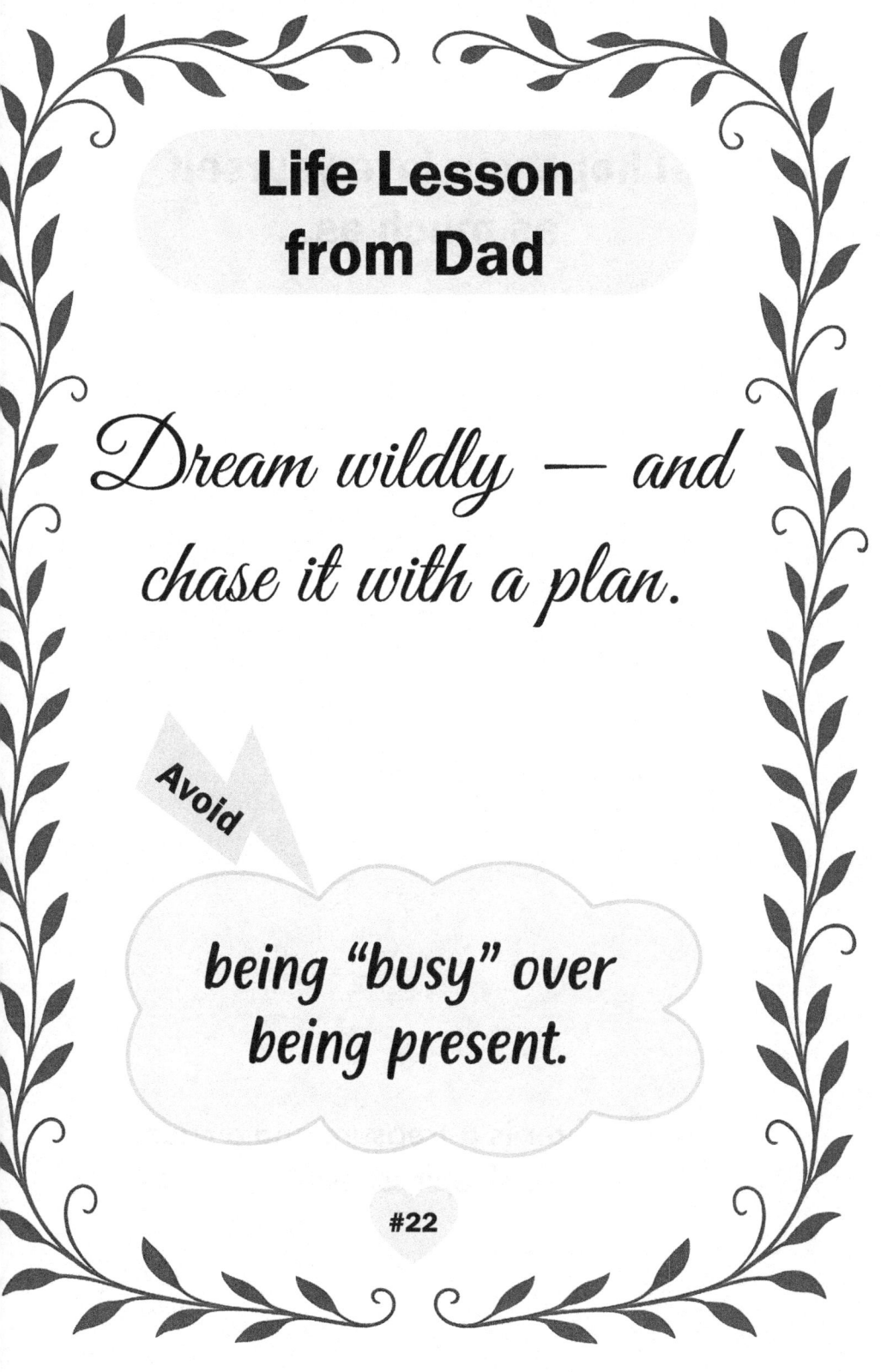

I hope you love yourself as much as...

"A daughter is a treasure and a cause of sleeplessness."
— Ben Sirach

Even when we don't agree, always know...

"Words are not enough to express the unconditional love that exists between a father and his daughter."

— Caitlin Houston

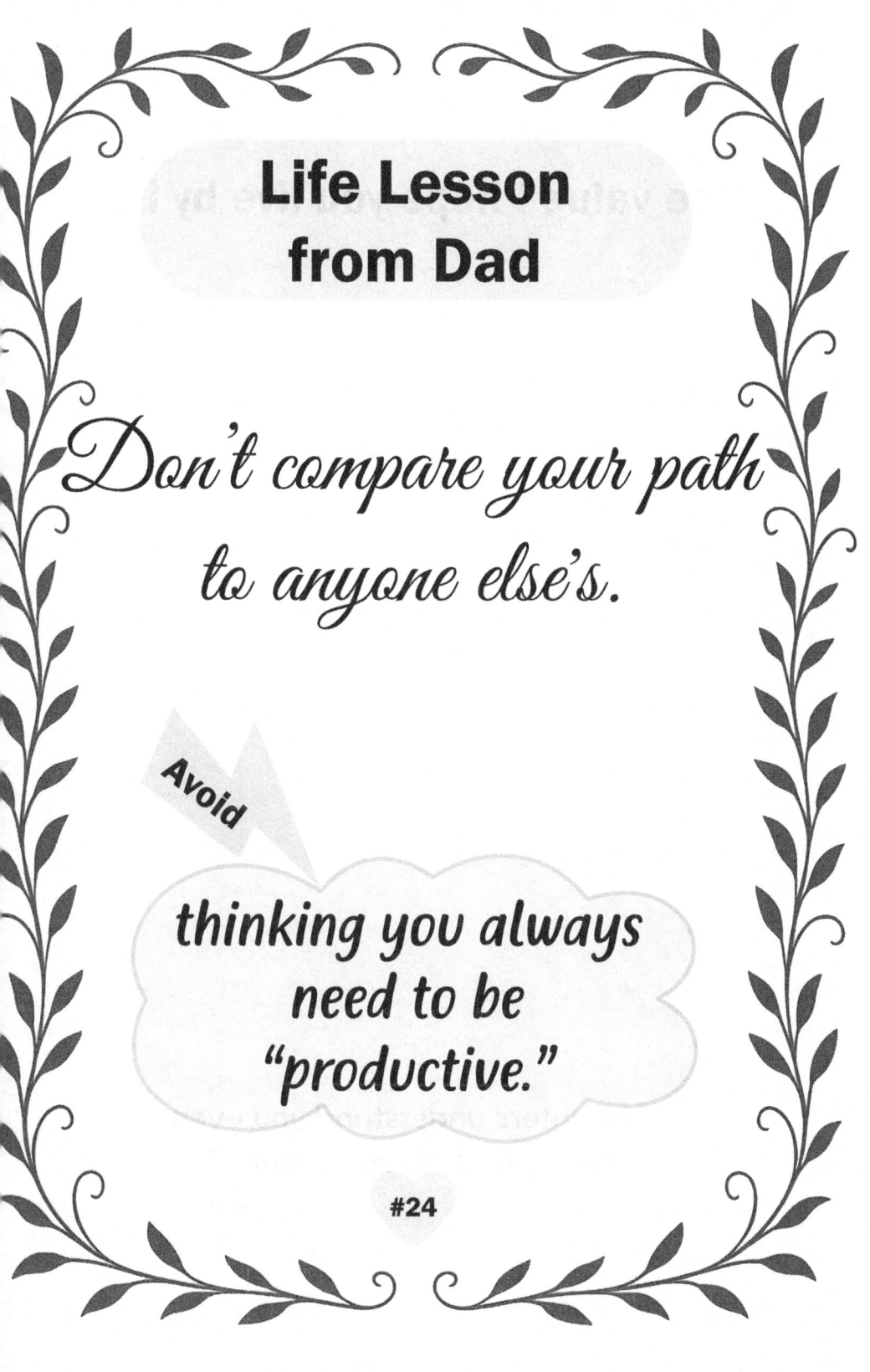

One value I hope you live by is...

"Daughters understand you even when you don't say a word."
— Unknown

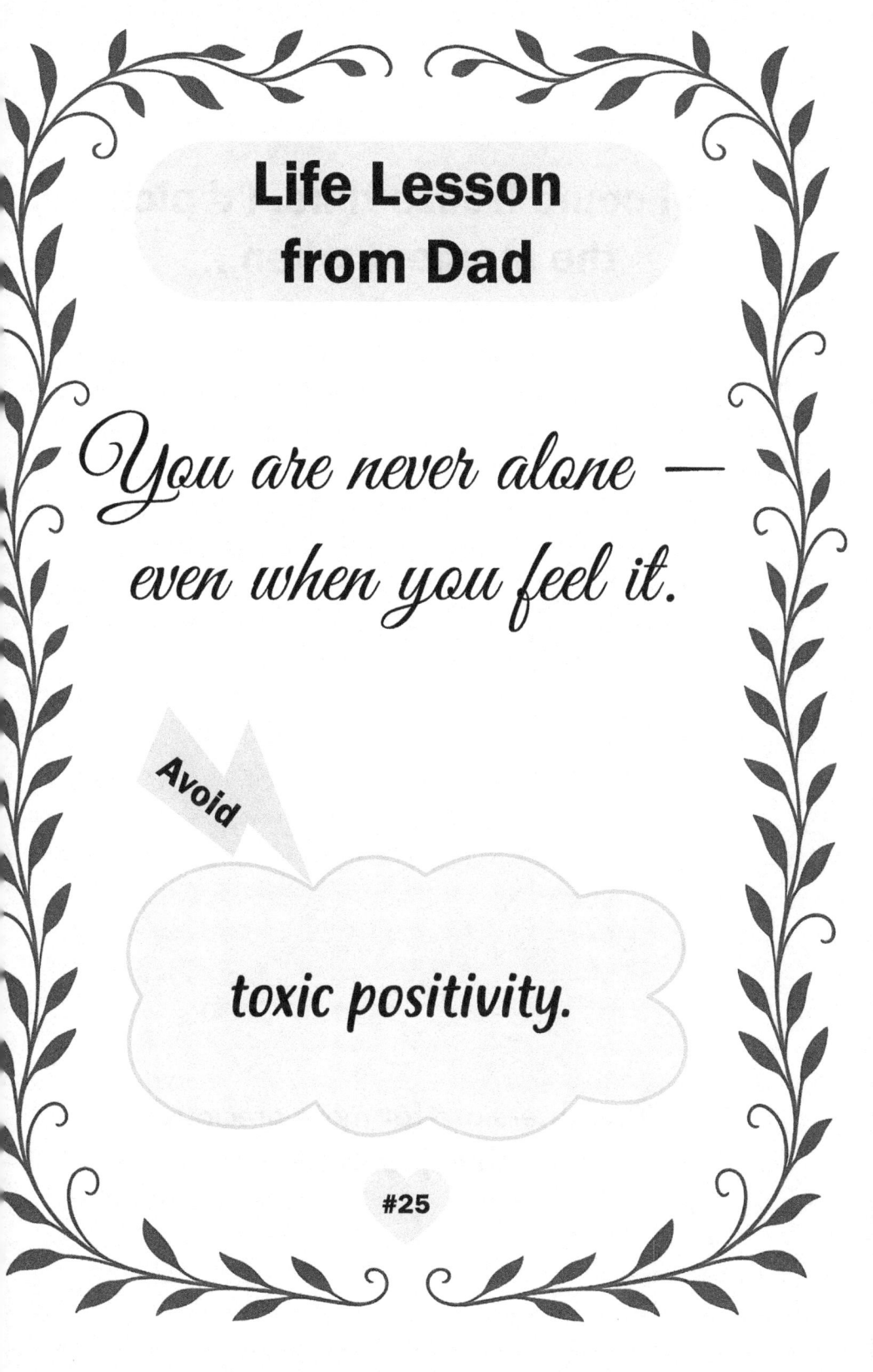

If I could freeze time, I'd pick the moment when...

"Daughters are far more precious than jewels."

— Bible, Proverbs 3:15 (paraphrased)

One thing I wish I had told you more often is...

"Every father should remember one day his son will follow his example, not his advice. But his daughter... she follows both."
— Unknown

When I think about your future, I imagine...

"A daughter is a bundle of firsts that excite and delight, giggles that come from deep inside, and always love."

— Barbara Cage

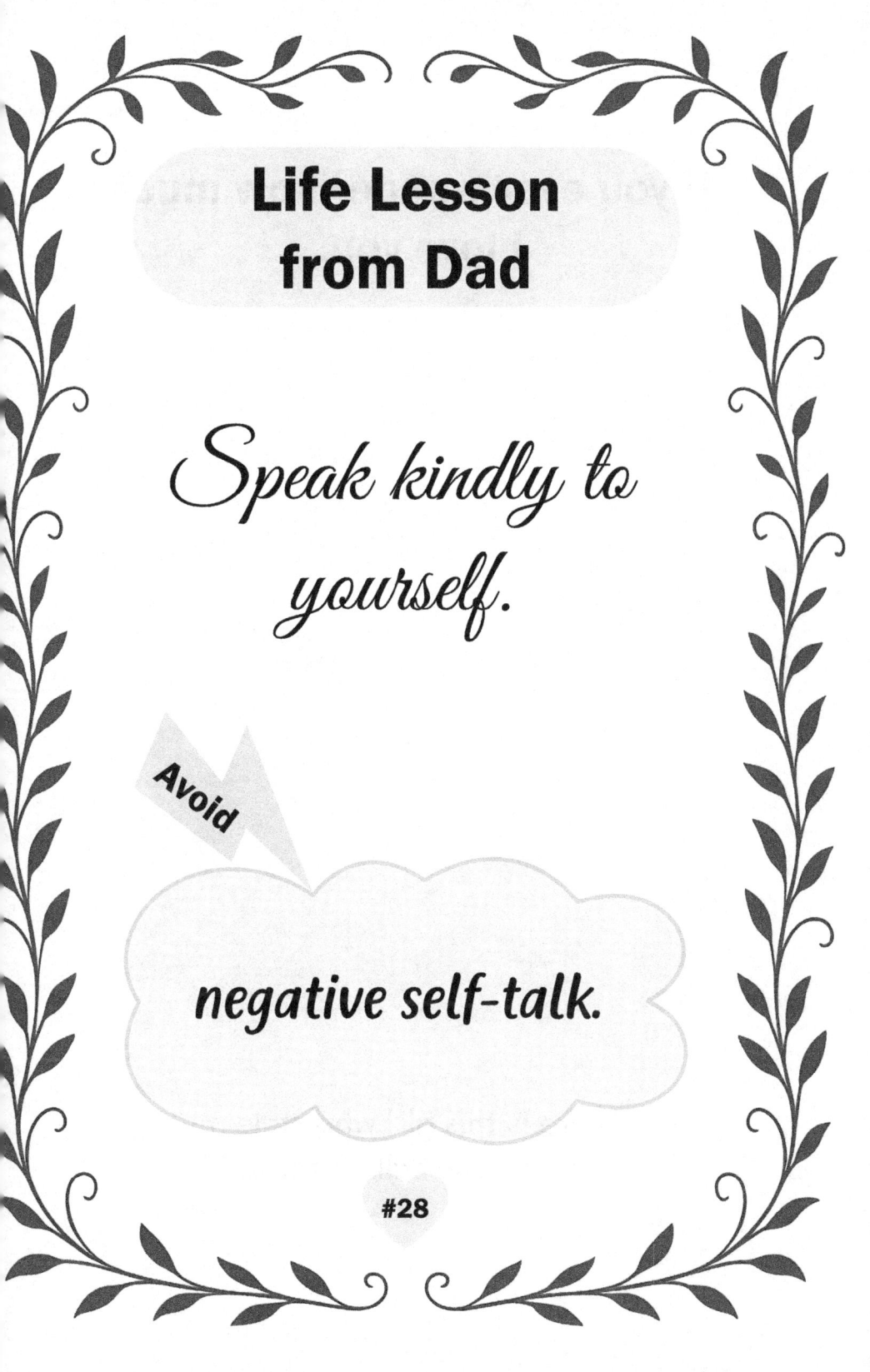

If you ever wonder how much I love you...

"There is this girl who stole my heart... she calls me Dad."

— Unknown

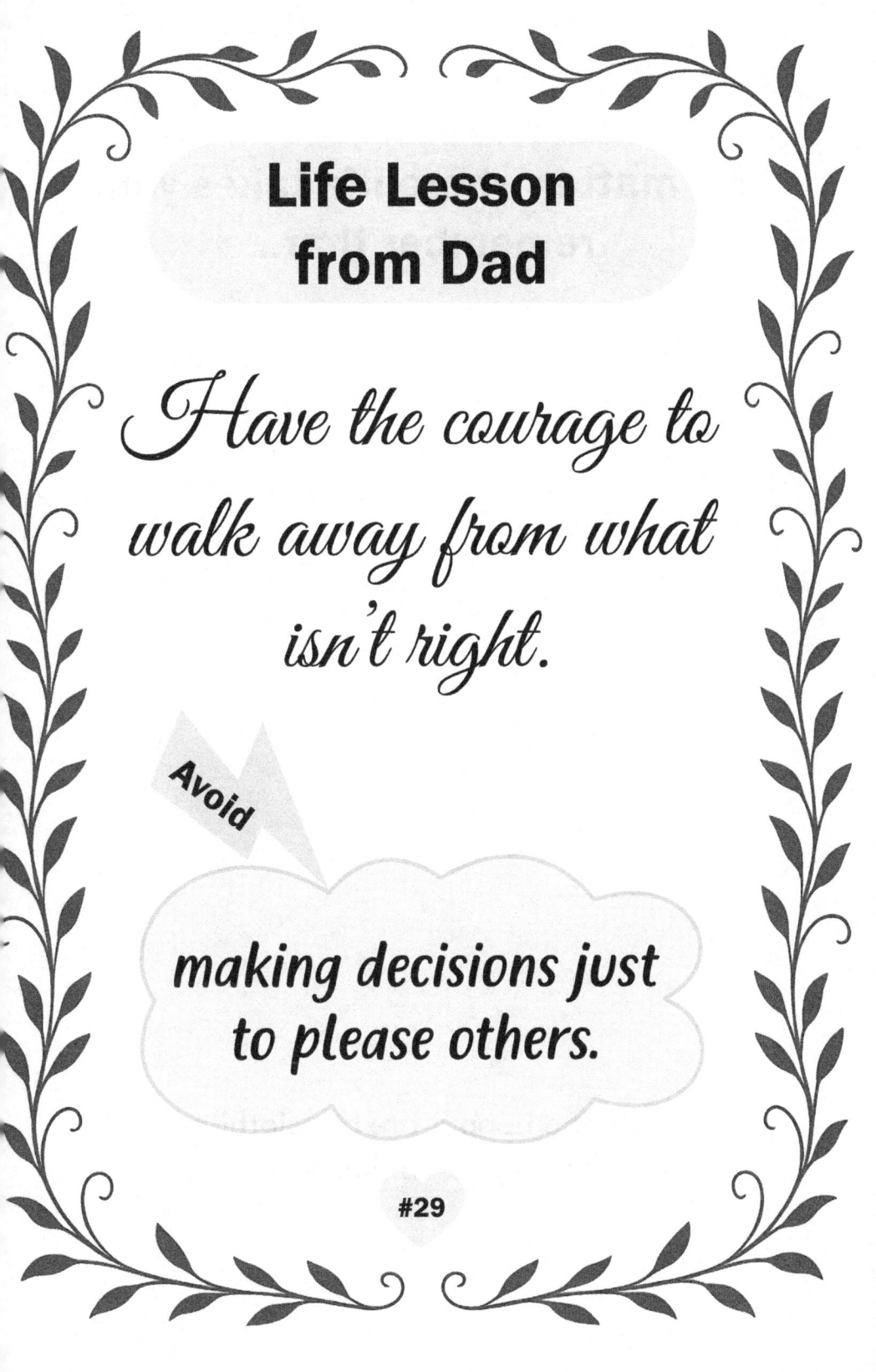

No matter where life takes you, remember that...

Strength and honour are her clothing; and she shall rejoice in time to come."

— Proverbs 31:25

The woman I see you becoming is...

"There is nothing quite like watching your baby girl grow into a beautiful woman."

— Colleen Oakes

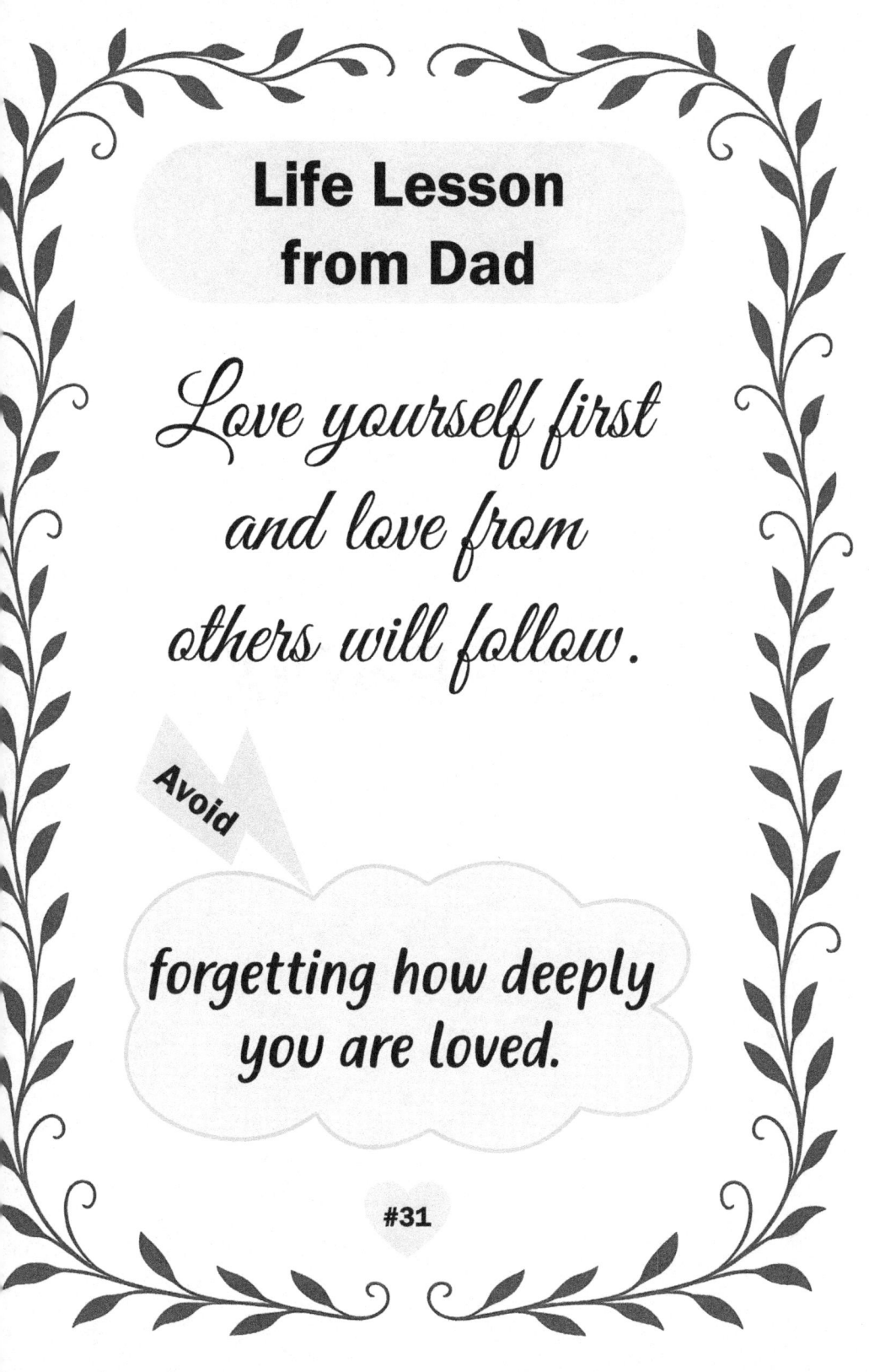

APPENDIX

Fatherly Goals I Commit to Do for You...

- ✓ Hold space for your dreams—even the ones you whisper softly.

- ✓ Protect you, whether you see it or not.

- ✓ Believe in you more fiercely than you sometimes believe in yourself.

- ✓ Listen, even when you don't have the words.

- ✓ Stay steady so you always know where "home" is.

- ✓ Let go when I need to, and hold on when you need me to.

- ✓ Smile at your happiness, even if it means hiding my tears.

- ✓ Quietly pray for your strength, peace, and joy.

- ✓ Forgive quickly, love deeply, and cheer endlessly.

- ✓ Love you unconditionally—with every part of who I am.

Being Your Father Means...

- ★ Killing spiders like it's my full-time job (no pay, no glory).

- ★ Pretending not to hear you call your mom when you're actually asking me to fix something.

- ★ Letting you have the last slice of pizza, even though I thought about it all day.

- ★ Instantly becoming a free Uber driver—with optional life lectures included.

- ★ Laughing at your jokes, even the ones I don't understand (which is... most).

- ★ Silently funding your snack addiction one "Target run" at a time.

- ★ Watching movies I didn't pick, with characters I don't know, in genres I don't like... because you're next to me.

- ★ Giving unsolicited but very correct advice you'll pretend to ignore.

- ★ Bragging about you to strangers in checkout lines like a proud maniac.

- ★ Loving you more than I can ever explain—no matter what, forever.

Special free bonus offer!

As our Thank You for getting this book, we want to give you access to a FREE new trivia game called **Brain Buzz Battle** for up to 8 players!

1. To receive a special advance copy of the next book, be sure to submit your email information using the link below.

2. Download it, print it, play it!

Register now at: **smartstarbooks.com**
Follow the link called "Free Bonus Game" gift offer.

www.SmartStarBooks.com

Please!

I'm asking you to please do me a favor and kindly leave an honest review of this book.

Amazon viewers value the opinions of other readers. Just follow the link or QR code and leave your review. I'd greatly appreciate it! THANK YOU very much.

- M. J. Cove

Link to review:

www.smartstarbooks.com/review-dad-to-daughter

or use the QR code link to review:

Made in the USA
Monee, IL
25 July 2025

21436100R00046